AF471987

Satan as Barack Obama

Stephen Kirk

AuthorHouse™
1663 Liberty Drive
Bloomington, IN 47403
www.authorhouse.com
Phone: 1-800-839-8640

First published by AuthorHouse 6/2/2011

ISBN: 978-1-4567-6382-4 (e)
ISBN: 978-1-4567-6384-8 (sc)

Library of Congress Control Number: 2011908381

Printed in the United States of America

LUKE 10:18
And He answered them,
“I beheld
Satan as Barack Obama
falling”.

Εἶπεν δὲ αὐτοῖς,

Ἐθεώρουν τὸν Σατανᾶν ὡς
ἀστραπὴν ἐκ τοῦ οὐρανοῦ
πεσόντα.

וַיַּעַן לָהֶם רָאִיתִי הַשָּׂטָן
כְּבָרָק וּבָמָה נוֹפֵל

Introduction

The United States of America has elected Barack Obama, the AntiChrist, to be the most powerful man in the world. I believe that Barack Obama does not know that he is the AntiChrist yet, he may never know that he is the Anti-Christ, he would probably scoff at this statement if presented, and yet the New Testament in the "red letter" words of Jesus calls Barack Obama by name as the persona of Satan at his falling.

The usual after church lunch discussions where Biblical eschatology is merged with current events has become NOW! The speculation about who is the Anti-Christ, or more correctly called the "Man of Lawlessness", has reached its conclusion.

This book will first walk the reader back through the basic simple Greek and Hebrew translations for the thirteen English words in the New King James Bible at Luke 10:18 which reveals "Barack Obama" as the phonetically uttered sounds from the lips of Jesus when He described His observation of Satan falling. This very logical step-by-step progression of translation from English to Greek and Greek to Hebrew will bring us to the name uttered as "Barack Obama" as Satan at his falling.

The second part of this book will describe the anti-Christ themes inherent in socialist governments of which Barack Obama and his cohorts are so fond. Using Judas Iscariot, the betrayer of Jesus as the archetype socialist amongst the apostles, this book will describe the sinister impacts and ungodly message that socialism brings to all peoples who succumb to its enticements.

The third part of this book will describe the effective end of the United States of America as we are removed from the world scene by a powerful nuclear holocaust which I suspect may be facilitated by Barack Obama, who is the Commander in Chief of all our nuclear force deterrents. Isaiah chapter 18 written in ~700 B.C. describes our country of Gentile believers who are cut down as a great nation with bodies left for the animals to devour, after which the chapter concludes that "In that time shall "The She" gift be brought unto the LORD of hosts of a people .... to the place of the name of the LORD of hosts, the Mount Zion." America, The Church, The Bride of Christ, this is your moment of disappearance from the awful tribulation to follow!

The final part will give a call to all believers for repentance and righteousness at this time. Lastly, for a book of this nature we must recognize that Christians are not called to rebel against a government based on anyone's prophetic message. Paul did not call for a war against Nero's Rome; rather, we are to submit to rulers within the bounds of Christian ethics and be at "Peace with all men as much as possible". All people who serve in the United States government are sworn to uphold the Constitution (not a particular person or his political party); therefore, let us all be reinvigorated to hold all who would support the "Man of Lawlessness" to a new level of scrutiny, transparency, and obedience to law.

Note these prophecies are not mine; they have been hidden as one of God's mysteries in scripture throughout the centuries with the key name "Barack Obama" coincidentally appearing on center stage at this day and time. Who better to receive the revelation of who the final Anti-Christ would be than Jesus, Himself? Even the Lord God per Revelation 13:18 desires us to figure out with wisdom the mark of the beast, which is the number of man, 666, the trinity of socialism (as if man can save himself!).

This book will not be structured like a work of fiction with a dramatic moment held off in secret to a climactic event. Rather I consider myself as a messenger on God's spiritual battlefield where my duties are to report to you, the "General of your life", as efficiently as possible that 1) a physical attack of immense magnitude is coming to America, 2) the strategy that the enemy is using to defeat God's people – socialism, and 3) the key commander of this assault – Barack Obama. As any good messenger I seek to communicate effectively, timely, and with supporting evidences for the decisions that you the "General" must make even though there will never be complete and perfect information (until we are on the other side of eternity).

This message of introduction/orientation is quickly followed as soon as possible by facts and conclusions. We shall therefore attempt to "make it plain that you may read it in a hurry"; there is no time for excuses.

> Then the LORD answered me and said: "Write the

> vision And make *it* plain on tablets, That he may run who reads it. [3] For the vision *is* yet for an appointed time; But at the end it will speak, and it will not lie. Though it tarries, wait for it; Because it will surely come, It will not tarry. [4] "Behold the proud, His soul is not upright in him; But the just shall live by his faith. (Hab 2:2-4 NKJ)

In essence, the audience needs to know the critical life & death decisions they are faced with. The remaining body of the text will provide the reader with their questions answered in a logical step-by-step fashion such that there will be no excuses left for avoiding the conclusion that Barack Obama is the Anti-Christ and the United States of America, as we now know it, is doomed to a catastrophic event of truly Biblical proportions. The audience is thus called out to be "His Church" and not worship the ways of this "Man of Lawlessness".

The Church is thus at war, but I would point out that when Jesus Christ's personal human family, John the Baptist his cousin, was beheaded by the "government Beast" of His day that Jesus did not declare a guerilla war. Rather He fought against His spiritual enemies by healing the masses from their spiritual lack:

> And Jesus, when He came out, saw a great multitude and was moved with compassion for them, because they were like sheep not having a shepherd. So He began to teach them many things. (Mark 6:34 NKJ)

I hope and pray that this book will likewise prepare the masses for a teachable moment before the harvest of America to the Lord's abode – Mount Zion.

Chapter 1

Did Jesus name the Anti-Christ?

Who other than Christ deserves better to have an answer to the question of "Who is the Anti-Christ?" or as the Bible specifically calls him the "Man of Lawlessness"?

Many things are included in the Bible as mysteries. However, they are mysteries to be uncovered at the appropriate time and place (e.g., the birth of the Messiah, the rebirth of Israel, the rise & fall of kingdoms). The purpose for mysteries with delayed revelation is after all necessary. If the Bible simply reported that the Anti-Christ will someday live at 1600 Pennsylvania Avenue and his name will be Barack Obama, then you can be assured that address and that child's name will never appear in the course of history. But God is staging the play, God is naming the characters, God is sequencing the acts --- all for the purposes of our understanding His glory and that we may partake of His heavenly reward of salvation through His Son Jesus Christ.

In 2nd Thessalonians 2:3-4 we are told that we can expect two signs of the end times - a) the great apostasy and b) the "Man of Lawlessness" revealed. Therefore, there will come a time when this revelation will occur although it has been hidden in the scriptures for centuries.

With that preface let us now take a look a Luke 10:18.

Examining Luke 10:18

First, Luke 10:18 is quite significant that this unusual statement by Jesus occurs sort of "out of the blue" as if Jesus has been relaxing and praying while his 70 disciples went out in pairs to spread the gospel.

The disciples return overjoyed that the demons are subject to them and share that with Jesus.

Then Jesus shares his revelation that must have occurred that same day, thus He says,

"I beheld Satan as ------ Barack Obama ----- falling."

Now the <u>sounds</u> "Barack Obama" would mean "lightning and high place" to these Hebrew disciples;

thus it would have meant "I beheld Satan as lightning and high place falling". Barack Obama was not a person to them for he had not yet appeared on the world stage!

NOTE: Bamah is the Hebrew word for the notorious "high places" where idol worship occurred in the Hebrew Old Testament. These "high places" (bamah) are mentioned hundreds of times. In our venacular it would have the dual meaning of saying that "Satan, the lightning (power) of the cultic place is falling".

When the Hebrew scribes put this into Greek they translated it as "I beheld Satan as lightning from heaven falling." I believe that they considered that the Greek word heaven was a suitable translation of the Hebrew "high place" especially since lightning comes from the clouds of heaven not mountains. The Hebrew word for heavens is "shamayim".

Therefore, it would be a typical scribal translation error to smooth out words to improve the logic/grammar/syntax of a Biblical verse as if to improve upon a "supposed" earlier error. Therefore, when there is a difference between Biblical text the "rougher translation" is actually preferred by scholars as being the most likely to be the true original. In essence, a scribe would not change a smooth wording to an unusual wording, since there is no purpose and no supposed improvement accomplished.[1] Of course, a scribe would logically be tempted to change the original "Barack Obama falling" pronunciation, since this does not indicate a person to the scribes. Instead this phrase simply means "lightning and high place falling" thus when the Hebrew is translated into Greek with a scribal smoothing it becomes "lightning from heaven falling".

A typical example of scribal smoothing is Mark 1:2 where two readings are found: (1) "as it is written in Isaiah the prophet" and (2) "as it is written in the prophets". The first reading is more firmly supported by the earlier manuscripts, but we can understand why a scribe would be tempted to change the reading because the text immediately following quotes both Isaiah and Malachi, not just Isaiah only.

Examples of Translation Smoothing

The most direct word for word translation of Luke 10:18 from the Greek to English is as discussed above:

And He answered them, *"I beheld Satan as lightning from heaven falling"*.

If we look at the various translations following we can see how some of the English translators moved the words around or changed word choices for their translation as best they saw fit:

(ASV) And he said unto them, I beheld Satan fallen as lightning from heaven.

(BBE) And he said, I was watching for Satan, falling from heaven like a star.

(CEV) Jesus told them: I saw Satan fall from heaven like a flash of lightning.

(DRB) And he said to them: I saw Satan like lightning falling from heaven.

(ESV) And he said to them, *"I saw Satan fall like lightning from heaven.*

(GNB) Jesus answered them, "I saw Satan fall like lightning from heaven.

(GW) Jesus said to them, "I watched Satan fall from heaven like lightning.

(ISV) He said to them, *"I was watching Satan fall from heaven like lightning.*

(KJV) And he said unto them, *I beheld Satan as lightning fall from heaven.*

(LITV) And He said to them, I saw Satan falling out of Heaven as lightning!

(MKJV) And He said to them, I saw Satan fall from Heaven like lightning.

(RV) And he said unto them, I beheld Satan fallen as lightning from heaven.

Now in reviewing the various translations of this single verse they are all true to the "concept" of the Greek words; however, only when we take those same Greek words in their original arrangement and translate them back into the Hebrew that would have been spoken by Jesus directly to His apostles do we get the key sounds of "Satan as Barack Obama". The intent here is to give one a flavor of how the rearrangement of words (which is often necessary in translation) can actually hide secrets that are not revealed until the end times. Such imperfect word-for-word translation rearrangements and scribal smoothing during translation as described above are all typical points of scholarly studies to find the original words of Jesus.

Jewish Idiom?

A reasonable question to ask would be, "Is this expression of lightning from heaven a Jewish idiom that has a completely different meaning than its physical description?" There is no reported scripture or other Aramaic/Hebrew idioms where Satan is referred to as lightning or associated with lightning. This of course is excluding the subject Luke 10:18 verse. I refer the reader to "Idioms in the Bible Explained and A Key to The Original Gospels" by George M. Lamsa, a man who grew up in a sheltered Middle East village speaking the same root Aramaic/Hebrew language as Jesus.[2] Lightning from heaven does not have a connotation of satanic evil. In fact, if anything lightning is associated with the power and displeasure of God per typical Western culture. "Lightning and High Place" or the pronunciation "Barack Obama" in Hebrew does not represent some kind of unique Jewish idiom with a special meaning.[3] We certainly have our own idioms such as saying "The man is in a pickle" which of course means "The man is in trouble". We even have descriptions for different types of falls. For example one could say:

a) I saw Satan as a "Ton of bricks" falling

b) I saw Satan as a "Dead duck" falling

c) I saw Satan as a "House of cards" falling

Would Jesus who is saying something very important here create his own idiom using "lightning" in the literal sense; thus leaving things to confusion? I think not!

Satan's Fall

Would there be significance to the lightning speed of Satan's falling? Satan's falling is a past event as described by Isaiah and Ezekiel below, therefore, I think not! For example below we see how Revelation recaps this event of Satan's fall. In fact, the phrase "from heaven" does not even fit here, since Satan has already been cast out of heaven shortly after the beginning of creation.

> "How you are fallen from heaven, O Lucifer, son of the morning! *How* you are cut down to the ground, You who weakened the nations! [13] For you have said

in your heart:`I will ascend into heaven, I will exalt my throne above the stars of God; I will also sit on the mount of the congregation On the farthest sides of the north; [14] I will ascend above the heights of the clouds, I will be like the Most High.' [15] Yet you shall be brought down to Sheol, To the lowest depths of the Pit. (Isa 14:12-14 NKJ)

"You *were* the anointed cherub who covers; I established you; You were on the holy mountain of God; You walked back and forth in the midst of fiery stones. [15] You *were* perfect in your ways from the day you were created, Till iniquity was found in you. [16] "By the abundance of your trading You became filled with violence within, And you sinned; Therefore I cast you as a profane thing Out of the mountain of God; And I destroyed you, O covering cherub, From the midst of the fiery stones. [17] "Your heart was lifted up because of your beauty; You corrupted your wisdom for the sake of your splendor; I cast you to the ground, I laid you before kings, That they might gaze at you. [18] "You defiled your sanctuaries By the multitude of your iniquities, By the iniquity of your trading; Therefore I brought fire from your midst; It devoured you, And I turned you to ashes upon the earth In the sight of all who saw you. (Eze 28:14-18 NKJ)

And war broke out in heaven: Michael and his angels fought with the dragon; and the dragon and his angels fought, [8] but they did not prevail, nor was a

> place found for them in heaven any longer. [9] So the great dragon was cast out, that serpent of old, called the Devil and Satan, who deceives the whole world; he was cast to the earth, and his angels were cast out with him. (Rev 12:7-9 NKJ)

Jesus and all his disciples would have surely known the fact that Satan had already been cast out of heaven at his fall – this is old news!

Therefore, for Luke 10:18 the statement beginning and ending words are not news "I beheld Satan as ________________ from heaven falling". It has the same excitement as someone today in 2011 standing up and saying "I beheld the Saints win the 2010 Super Bowl" to which most of us would reply --- "Well, good for you!". This event is past history – anyone can rent the CD!

Now if Jesus was saying that He was there <u>in heaven</u> when Satan was thrown out, then He would essentially be declaring Himself as God in heaven. Some of the Saints fans in the 2010 Super Bowl likely thought they had died and gone to heaven and likewise wanted to brag to everyone that they were there! However, though we know Jesus was in heaven when Satan was thrown out and though we know Jesus is a "saints" fan I just cannot see Him bragging about being there when "war broke out in heaven" (Rev 12:7)!

NOTE: Saints is the translation of "holy ones" – God's people, not necessarily the Black & Gold NFL team!

Prior to Barack Obama

In the past when reading the Luke 10:18 scripture it is certainly acceptable to consider the "lightning from heaven" as a simile for the activities in the spiritual dimension that the disciples accomplished with their recent ministry. Matthew Henry's commentary on Luke 10:18 listed below is certainly a valid example assessment:

> He confirmed what they said, as agreeing with his own observation (Luk_10:18): "My heart and eye went along with you; I took notice of the success you had, and I *saw Satan fall as lightning from heaven.*" Note, Satan and his kingdom fell before the preaching of the gospel. "I see how it is," saith Christ, "as you get ground the devil loseth ground." He falls *as lightning falls from heaven,* so suddenly, so irrecoverably, so visibly, that all may perceive it, and say, "See how Satan's kingdom totters, see how it tumbles." They triumphed in casting devils out of the bodies of people; but Christ sees and rejoices in the fall of the devil from the interest he has in the souls of men, which is called his power *in high places,* Eph_6:12. He foresees this to be but an earnest of what should now be shortly done and was already begun - the destroying of Satan's kingdom in the world by the extirpating of idolatry and the turning of the nations to the faith of Christ. Satan *falls from heaven* when he falls from the throne in men's hearts, Act_26:18. And Christ foresaw that the preaching of the gospel, which would *fly like lightning* through the world,

> would wherever it went pull down Satan's kingdom. *Now is the prince of this world cast out.* Some have given another sense of this, as looking back to the fall of the angels, and designed for a caution to these disciples, lest their success should puff them up with pride: "I saw angels turned into devils by *pride:* that was the sin for which Satan was *cast down from heaven,* where he had been an angel of light I saw it, and give you an intimation of it lest you, being *lifted up with pride should fall into that condemnation of the devil,* who fell by pride," 1Ti_3:6.

I therefore consider this Luke 10:18 a verse that is designed by God to for a time conceal the name of Barack Obama in an apparently innocuous comment by Jesus, but then upon his appearance on planet earth as the head of the most powerful nation on earth, to allow for his exposure as the soon to be Anti-Christ.

This is all part of God's plans to reveal His mysteries at the appointed times. Other verses where God has hidden future revelations in scripture are exampled by Isaiah chapter 53 which describes the crucifixion of Christ, yet was unrecognized by the Jewish scholars of His day. Additionally, the final chapters of this very book will describe how Isaiah chapter 18 describes the destruction of the United States of America, yet is also largely unrecognized today. The lesson that we all must learn is that scripture as God's Word, truly contains treasure maps of value beyond measure.

Ehud Barak – Israeli Minister of Defense

There are certainly other Barack/Barak(s) in this world. After all Barak was the name of an Old Testament military hero (Judges chapters 4-5). The current Minister of Defense for Israel and former Prime Minister of Israel is named Ehud Barak. He also is a man of political power with multitudes of nuclear weapons at his disposal. Could this Luke 10:18 verse apply to Ehud Barak? Could Jesus have been saying the following?,

A) "I beheld Satan as (Ehud) Barak from heaven falling"

Or as I have proposed in the original Hebrew phonetics,

b) "I beheld Satan as (Ehud) Barak and high place falling"

In case A this version would not make sense because Ehud Barak has never been in heaven thus he cannot fall from heaven. In case B though physically possible for Ehud and a high place to fall it does not make sense in that Israelites today are not going to the high places to formally worship false gods. Nor for that matter were the Jews of Jesus day going to the high places to worship. The false idol worship was cleared up by God allowing the Babylonian conquest and enslavement of Israel in 597 B.C. Therefore, we can make the following exclusions for the phonetic words following "Barack" in Jesus statement:

1) Heaven is excluded because it is old news as described above

2) High Place is excluded because at the time of Christ the Jewish nation was not fraught with the issues of idol worship at the high places (i.e., bamah) like they did before the Babylonian captivity

Thus we are left with the Hebrew statement by Jesus:

"I beheld Satan as Barack Obama falling".

Further Evidences

In summary, Luke 10:18 without the name Barack Obama in it is a statement that is not worthy of the significant "pause for attention" given it during the great return celebration of the disciples from casting out demons and healing the sick. However, when this blank is filled in with the Hebrew translation for lightning, "Barack", the current day implications call for a deep time of intercession with God. Even God, Himself says to ask Him for wisdom in spiritual matters:

> If any of you lacks wisdom, let him ask of God, who gives to all liberally and without reproach, and it will be given to him. (Jam 1:5 NKJ)

When the correction to the translation synonym of high place instead of heaven is made, "bamah", then we have reached an astounding revelation of a Biblical mystery. Note how in Isaiah 14:13-14 we can see how the ancient Hebrew writers interchangeably used heaven and heights or "shamayim and bamah" to express the same concept in repetition for emphasis (**bold** Hebrew pronunciations are by the author):

> For you have said in your heart:`I will ascend into heaven **(shamayim)**, I will exalt my throne above the stars of God; I will also sit on the mount of the congregation On the farthest sides of the north; [14] I will ascend above the heights **(bamah)** of the clouds, I will be like the Most High.' (Isa 14:13-14 NKJ)

Given the similarity of concept here, then we can see how a scribe confronted with the apparent Hebrew statement:

"I beheld Satan as lightning and high place falling"

would be logical in his "smoothing" of the translation into Greek by reporting the text as:

"I beheld Satan as lightning from heaven falling"

Little did he know that "lightning and high place" in Hebrew translate to "Barack Obama" the 44th President of the United States.

Now can we know the significance and meaning of Luke 10:18 and why this curious verse would be recorded though possibly not fully understood by the apostles. I believe the emotional implications of this statement's moment were passed on to the disciples such that they did remember and did record it into Greek as best they knew. Certainly God is the revealer of His mysteries and He has the Director's right to conceal through the centuries and then reveal at His time to those He desires. Agatha Christie's mysteries would likewise have less impact if all the clues were revealed immediately from the start with no mind searching required by the audience. Jesus deliberately gave us instructions to "seek and you shall find", "knock and the door will be opened" because He knew that until we ask, search, open we have not made room for the answer!

In Jesus's word to the apostles He said:

> "But the Helper, the Holy Spirit, whom the Father will send in My name, He will teach you all things, and bring to your remembrance all things that I said to you. (John 14:26 NKJ)

Jesus Revelation Excitement

The revelation that Barack Obama is the Anti-Christ, the Man of Lawlessness, who will be empowered by Satan to deceive the nations, is significant. If this key individual of end times eschatology has just been revealed to Jesus, then the pause that he provides to announce and thus eventually have recorded in scripture the name of the Anti-Christ, then that is worth millions of souls in our end times generation. We must get the message out!

It is also noteworthy that immediately afterward (within the hour) that Jesus makes a statement of how significant the revelation is that these disciple "babes" have just heard.

> In that hour Jesus rejoiced in the Spirit and said, "I thank You, Father, Lord of heaven and earth, that You have hidden these things from *the* wise and prudent and revealed them to babes. Even so, Father, for so it seemed good in Your sight. [22] "All things have been delivered to Me by My Father, and no one knows who the Son is except the Father, and who the Father is except the Son, and *the one* to whom the Son wills to reveal *Him*." [23] Then He turned to *His* disciples and said privately, "Blessed *are* the eyes which see the things you see; [24] "for I tell you that many prophets and kings have desired to see what you see, and have not seen *it*, and to hear what you hear, and have not heard *it*." (Luk 10:21-24 NKJ)

Obviously, something significant was said here by Jesus! It was revealed to babes indicating there was at least some lack of understanding by the disciples. We likewise today need to listen and hear what the Lord Jesus is saying here. Certainly many centuries of scriptural study have been exercised toward the answer to the question of "Who is the Anti-Christ?". Therefore, again the words of Jesus fit with the message and emotion that would be carried with this AntiChrist revelation.

Hebrew Translation of Barack Obama

Now for a small amount of Hebrew translation and pronunciation mentoring to see how the English "lightning and high place" becomes "Barack Obama" when translated into Hebrew. The Luke 10:18 verse is only thirteen English words long and we will not translate all thirteen, rather we will leave them as is. Appendix A lists the key Hebrew words including their pronunciation and meaning for the readers direct comparison. Please note the following:

1) The Baraq or Barack (as we would pronounce it) is the Hebrew pronunciation for lightning. This is thus a very straight-forward translation. What a coincidence that the name given to the most powerful man in the world is linked to Satan in the Luke 10:18 verse. Even just the first part of the Luke 10:18 verse is unnerving "I watched Satan as Barack.......falling".

2) Throughout scripture "the high place(s)" of cultic worship are pronounced " habamah" (the first " ha" is "the" in Hebrew. The "a" are all pronounced like the "a" in father.

3) The Hebrew "vav" conjunction for "and" is pronounced as a "u/oo" when it is before a Hebrew letter "bet" or the equivalent of an English "b".

Since nowhere else in scripture is lightning related to Satan, then I think this curious statement from Jesus was "I beheld Satan, as Barack Obama, falling".

NOTE: I also find it also quite coincidental that Barack's first Chief of Staff Rahm Emanuel is Jewish and his name Rahm means "Thunder" --- Is God telling us something when "Lightning and Thunder" are the two most powerful men in the world (and they are ungodly)! Is God telling us something when America's deadliest enemy, Osama, rhythms with Obama! Anyone who knows the Bible knows how critical and meaningful the names are that God gives to the key actors across His stage of history -- He wants us to get the message; whatever it takes!

Satan and Anti-Christ linked

Let us now briefly look at one example of how Satan is tied with the Anti-Christ.

> Then I saw another beast coming up out of the earth, and he had two horns like a lamb and spoke like a dragon. [12] And he exercises all the authority of the first beast in his presence, and causes the earth and those who dwell in it to worship the first beast, whose deadly wound was healed. [13] He performs great signs, so that he even makes fire come down from heaven on the earth in the sight of men. [14] And he deceives those who dwell on the earth by those signs which he was granted to do in the sight of the beast, telling those who dwell on the earth to make an image to the beast who was wounded by the

> sword and lived. (Rev 13:11-14 NKJ)

In summary, scripture prophesizes that there will be in the future a leader of governmental power (i.e, a beast) who will be wounded to near death, yet miraculously recover. This person will then be fully empowered by the dragon from the Abyss to do signs and wonders to deceive the masses. Satan, the dragon, therefore counterfeits the true resurrection of Jesus Christ through the Anti-Christ even to the point of causing the earth to worship this "supposedly resurrected" government leader. As Jesus himself stated "I beheld Satan as Barack...... falling!" and this fall of course describes how at the end the Anti-Christ will be cast into hell.

> The devil, who deceived them, was cast into the lake of fire and brimstone where the beast and the false prophet *are*. And they will be tormented day and night forever and ever. (Rev 20:10 NKJ)

What is one to think when the words of Jesus link the name Barack with Satan? Barack Obama, is the commander-in-chief of the most powerful nation on earth. Barack is a man with a godless mother and a communist father who abandoned him. Barack was a young child who was immersed in Muslim training during his most critical formative years. He is a man who only in his later years (after considering his political positioning) decided to publicly claim Christianity as his faith. Barack is a man who sat for years under the spiritual leadership of a "Liberation Theology" pastor spewing out epithets cursing America. He is a man who is cunningly deceptive with his words. He is a man whose faith is in people and government controls rather than God. Barack Obama represents the perfect example and background to fill the role of the end times Anti-Christ.

Appendix A lists the key Hebrew words referenced above which are taken direct from Strong's Concordance and Holladay's Lexicon[4] which are both Biblical reference standards having decades of usage.

Chapter 2
What are the odds?

The Lord God can certainly call out the name of men before they are on the stage of history. For example, Cyrus, a pagan, a tribal leader called to be the future king of Persia, was named by God to do his bidding for the conquering of Babylon, the most powerful nation on earth. At the time of this Isaiah prophecy Israel had not even been conquered by Babylon and the temple had not been destroyed.

> **Isa 44:28** Who says of Cyrus, *'He is* My shepherd, And he shall perform all My pleasure, Saying to Jerusalem, "You shall be built," And to the temple, "Your foundation shall be laid."'

> **Isa 45:1** "Thus says the LORD to His anointed, To Cyrus, whose right hand I have held— To subdue nations before him And loose the armor of kings, To

open before him the double doors, So that the gates will not be shut:

Isa 45:2 ' I will go before you And make the crooked places straight; I will break in pieces the gates of bronze And cut the bars of iron.

Isa 45:3 I will give you the treasures of darkness And hidden riches of secret places, That you may know that I, the LORD, Who call *you* by your name, *Am* the God of Israel.

Isa 45:4 For Jacob My servant's sake, And Israel My elect, I have even called you by your name; I have named you, though you have not known Me.

Isa 45:5 I *am* the LORD, and *there is* no other; *There is* no God besides Me. I will gird you, though you have not known Me,

Isa 45:6 That they may know from the rising of the sun to its setting That *there is* none besides Me. I *am* the LORD, and *there is* no other; (NKJ)

Given the horror of accepting Barack Obama as the Anti-Christ may push many people into a dismissive response saying, "Well that is just an interesting coincidence!". Most people do not want their lives interrupted with inconveniences much less global destruction and tribulation. However, if we want to be clear thinking especially about such emotional issues then we need to put our information to logical tests. There are three types of logical arguments – deductive, inductive, and abductive.

Deductive arguments approach the decision making process essentially like a geometric proof. The following is a classic example:

All men are mortal.

The Anti-Christ is a man.

The Anti-Christ will die.

However, though exact and essentially producing guaranteed conclusions the deductive arguments apply to very few real world cases.

Inductive arguments are constructed in such as way as to produce conclusions that follow only probably from the premises. Unlike deductive arguments, inductive arguments cannot guarantee the truth of a conclusion. A strong inductive argument offers enough evidence to make the conclusion likely (or highly likely). While deductive arguments by definition lack certainty, in most real life situations, probability is the best a person can hope for.[5] Ken Samples in his book "A World of Difference – Putting Christian Truth-Claims to the Worldview Test" provides this inductive argument example:

Adolf Hitler was a dictator and an evil man.

Hideki Tojo was a dictator and an evil man.

Benito Mussolini was a dictator and an evil man.

Joseph Stalin was a dictator and an evil man.

Mao Tse-tung was a dictator and an evil man.

Kim Il Sung was a dictator and an evil man.

Idi Amin was a dictator and an evil man.

Pol Pot was a dictator and an evil man.

Saddam Hussein was a dictator and an evil man.

Therefore, it is highly likely that the next dictator (e.g., Anti-Christ) to appear on the world scene will be an evil man.

Probability is a tool that can tell us whether something is a coincidence or beyond coincidence indicating a specific design by a mind. For example, we all use passwords of a specific length and complexity so that we can know that we are protected. Appendix B demonstrates how we can know that this specified complexity in names, sentences, and entire books of genetic information is indicative of a designers mind not just attributable to random coincidence. As an engineer with some BioChemical engineering background I know that clients do not pay for "random engineering" because it does not and cannot produce anything of value. I find it sad that many people just don't do the math to provide themselves with ordered thinking and see for themselves the fingerprints of God upon the Universe as the Ultimate Mind and Creator. Literally, the evidence of design in creation is so strong that one would have to be monstrously bigoted against God to conclude otherwise (See Romans 1:20-22). Sadly some are so disappointed that God did not create them and the universe to please "their standards" that they have adopted the philosophy of "Anything but God or else a god that suits their ego!".

Obviously, God could not spell out "Barack Hussein Obama at 1600 Pennsylvania Avenue is the Anti-Christ" since that would be quite a definitively long password to know who the Anti-Christ is. However, one could say that by giving us the definitive name of Barack Obama linked to Satan as described in Chapter 1 then he has given us the wisdom to understand who the AntiChrist is.

What about 666?

As God calls out in Revelation 13:18 below He wants us to figure/ calculate these things out:

> Here is wisdom. Let him who has understanding calculate the number of the beast, for it is the number of a man: His number *is* 666. (Rev 13:18 NKJ)

Note carefully above that when the indefinite article "a" is removed from the translation before the "man", then the meaning takes on the better translation below:

> This calls for wisdom. Let the person who has insight calculate the number of the beast, for it is humanities number. That number is 666. (Rev 13:18 NIV 2010)

The indefinite article "a" is not there in the Greek. It simply states "the number of man" when translated directly thus the NIV translation from Greek to English is superior. This, of course, changes the picture in that we are no longer looking for a particular, symbol, number, name, rather we are looking for a "philosophy concept" that is based on man to the obvious exclusion of God. As Riddlebarger in "The Man of Sin" citing the work of Beale states:[6]

"The omission of the article in Revelation 13:18 indicates the general idea of humanity, not some special individual who can be discerned only through an esoteric method of calculation. Therefore, in both verses ἀνθρώπου [man] is a descriptive or qualitative genitive, so that the phrase here should be rendered 'a human number' or 'a number of humanity'. It is a number common to fallen humanity."

To the extent that Islamic terrorism continues to force more and more aggressive security measures then we should not be surprised at whatever mark or other security devices may someday be employed upon hands and foreheads in order to allow the government beast to control the world's peoples and enforce his loyal worship. In summary, we must beware of a godless socialist system that controls the preponderance of the economy by whatever security means it deems necessary. Who does this sound like to you?

The next chapter will discuss how we have betrayed ourselves and God through socialism.

666 – A History of Intrigue

I write this book knowing that for years the world has sought ways to stick the label of 666 on every leader that they could. My apologies to Ronald Reagan and others who have suffered at the ignorance of Christians that did not take the time to carefully read their own instruction manuals, the Bible. All I can do here is humbly report my research into the actual Greek, translations from Greek back to Hebrew with likely scribal smoothing, and the results that spell out Barack Obama.

I believe I am obedient to the call of Revelation 13:18, especially since when this verse is amplified for its fuller meanings as shown below it clearly indicates that this determination will require some stepwise, methodical thinking processes. Therefore, no apologies need be given for the fact that the revealing of the name of the Anti-

Christ, Barack Obama, is a multi-step process. This book is definitely a process of feeling and searching in English, Greek, and Hebrew.

> This calls for wisdom. Let the person who has insight *(intellect, mind, understanding)* calculate *(manipulate, verify by contact; figuratively to search for: - feel after, handle, touch)* the number *(a number (as reckoned up))* of the beast, for it is humanities number. (Rev 13:18 NIV 2010 with amplification)

Therefore, I conclude that the meaning of 666 is relatively simple as the number of man (i.e., salvation by socialism), but the ferreting out of the name of the person of the Anti-Christ beast requires some effort or "reckoning up" as described above, but this "search" is within the bounds of normal scriptural text experience.

In summary, as the public is fond of saying "I would not vote for Barack Obama even if he ran for dog catcher." Personally, even if he was the most godly, conservative, red, white, & blue American on the public stage I would not be able to vote for him because his name is literally linked to the persona of Satan direct from the lips of Jesus. Surely, America can find someone else to elect, regardless of one's political preferences, other than an individual whose name is scripturally linked to Satan. Only someone with a narcissistic, Anti-Christ personality would consider themselves indispensable.

Chapter 3

Socialism: The Christ Betrayers

Worship God; not Gov(ernment)

“If God can’t get it done with his church, then I will get it done with my political power!” Such is the heartfelt internal cry within so many of us.

Does that sound like a slap in the face of God or what?

Using the government to force people to pay for what some consider their “God given” rights removes 1) the dignity of the giver as well as 2) the glory of God to work in the spiritual lives of individual donors. Such mandated social engineering practices like Prohibition are fraught with pitfalls. Prohibition brought the Mafia to America, thus strengthening God’s enemies.

If mankind becomes dependent on "other mankind" to meet their needs, then does man have any further use for God? Shall we become as unbridled as Sodom & Gomorrah (Ezekiel 16:49) once we have all our needs met without God? Is dependence on God a bad thing that must be wiped from the face of the earth as being somehow the final plague of mankind? I think the socialist mindset will surprisingly answer "Yes" when taken to its full conclusion.

The efforts by social engineers to do more than the minimum government requirements truly represents the outgrowth of a "transference neurosis". Certain individuals who during their formative years felt "out of control" due to abandonment by parents or who felt a burden of social outcasting due to inferiority complexes, etc. can become obsessed with having control over their lives and even control over the lives of others by extension of their overwhelming fears. Such individuals are prone to gravitate toward politics as the ultimate controller of life and security. Add a touch of narcissism developed from a parent who repeatedly stressed to a child their elite uniqueness relative to others and we have the set up for a Barack Obama political personality. [7]

God instituted government, but government is instituted to do only a few things:

- Protect the individual and society from physical oppression by the more powerful (military, police)

- Provide protection from monopolistic activities that thwart freedom, enterprise, and commerce (i.e., Tower of Babylon was man's 1st attempt to monopolize/control mankind and his communication systems)

- Provide minimal administrative services (i.e., tax collection, notary services for contracts, prisons)

- Provide for the judicial system to implement criminal and civil restitutions and punishments

- Provide for the care/protection of those incapable mentally to make their own decisions (e.g., children, elderly, insane); however, this care and support is only provided as a last resort since it represents the removal of such citizens rights of freedom

Note the religious requirements relative to Israel's special covenant with God are omitted here, since that is a separate religious subject matter.

Judas Iscariot: The Socialism Betrayer of Christ

Why do I bring the issues and discussion of social engineering into the discussion of this book?

Because as we look to Judas Iscariot, as the archetype betrayer of Jesus Christ, it is not for the pleasure of wine, drugs, and drunkenness that he betrays Christ, it is not for jealousy of Christ abilities that he betrays Christ, it is not for any type of adultery related intrigue that he betrays Christ, it is not because of a specific religious disagreement with Christ, rather we can see in Judas Iscariot the uncontrolled rejection of Christ because he did not direct His financial resources/ gifts to the poor.

Just think Simon the Israeli nationalist zealot could have slit Jesus throat because he did not wipe out the Romans! Matthew, the tax collector, could have turned Jesus into the Roman authorities for a nice whistle blower bonus, if he failed to pay tax on the wealth donated to His ministry! James and John, the sons of Thunder, whose mother wanted them to be seated on the right and left hand of Jesus in His glory could have assassinated him when He refused! Peter could have knifed Jesus for calling Him a coward that would deny Him before all the other disciples! These disciples had all the bad habits of many church people today! Yet – for all of their failings none but Judas Iscariot held on to his "disappointment with God" to the point of betrayal. How many people stay outside the bounds of God's love because they are somehow, someway disappointed in God!

I find it interesting how many of those actually in poverty will live their life in contentment and with a full faith toward God; yet it is those who are empowered with wealth and status who are often more concerned than the impoverished. These faithless persons concern is not for the poor, rather it is the concern that they themselves will become the poor and thus "out-of-control". Of course without wealth and without God, then this existence becomes death in their eyes.

The original temptation in the Garden of Eden was all about control, all about being "like God". The grasping to be God, the jealousy against One with a higher position is what caused Satan to be cast down from heaven in the first place.

I like Dr. D. James Kennedy's definition for socialism, "Socialism is legalized plundering!". God did not make us all the same and only an Anti-Christ government beast would try to make us all the same! My nightmare vision of socialism is a line of hundreds of people standing in the cold all waiting for hours on a mean-spirited bureaucrat at the end of the line who will issue size ten shoes to everyone no matter their foot size. I contrast that with a fully stocked Walmart in the

USA and my choices are clear! How easy it is to forget that mankind has practiced free enterprise trade in villages of all cultures since the beginning of time--- without government interference!

Judas: Blinded by Social Inequalities

Below is a chronology of key events regarding Judas Iscariot through the gospels. I believe it is insightful to see how this antiChrist among the disciples played out his life.

> And being in Bethany at the house of Simon the leper, as He sat at the table, a woman came having an alabaster flask of very costly oil of spikenard. Then she broke the flask and poured *it* on His head. (Mar 14:3 NKJ)

Note that this critical event which will turn Judas against Christ occurs in Simon the leper's house. It is interesting that Judas is listed as Simon's son in the verse below. I wonder if Judas became passionate to the point of anger because at one time may be he too was concerned that he may become a leper like Simon. Was this the reason for Judas having a "disappointment with God" attitude? Simon himself had a dismissive attitude toward Jesus (Luke 7:36-50). The fact that Simon is described as a leper and the fact that Israelites were prohibited from being in the house of a leper, then this further stresses the irony of a man healed from leprosy yet who fails to be thankful to the Healer. Jesus made a point of stressing how a foreigner Samaritan leper returned to thank Jesus for his healing (Luke 17:11-19), but the other nine did not thank Him. Simon by contrast was himself a Pharisee. When Judas saw the ointment poured out on Christ I wonder if he viewed that as his potential healing ointment (e.g., Obama healthcare) disappearing before his eyes?

We are all concerned about our health; the subject touches us all at a very personal level. Therefore, I intentionally focus toward this illustrative event that is recorded in the Bible which marks the emotions of the very man that betrayed Jesus Christ. Have we let our emotions similarly blind us?

> Then one of His disciples, Judas Iscariot, Simon's
> *son*, who would betray Him, said, [5] "Why was this
> fragrant oil not sold for three hundred denarii (i.e., a
> year's wages) and given to the poor?" [6] This he said,
> not that he cared for the poor, but because he was
> a thief, and had the money box; and he used to take
> what was put in it. (Joh 12:4-6 NKJ)

> But Jesus said, "Let her alone. Why do you trouble
> her? She has done a good work for Me. [7] "For you
> have the poor with you always, and whenever you
> wish you may do them good; but Me you do not
> have always. [8] "She has done what she could. She
> has come beforehand to anoint My body for burial.
> [9] "Assuredly, I say to you, wherever this gospel is
> preached in the whole world, what this woman
> has done will also be told as a memorial to her."
> (Mar 14:6-9 NKJ)

> Then Satan entered Judas, surnamed Iscariot, who
> was numbered among the twelve. [4] So he went
> his way and conferred with the chief priests and
> captains, how he might betray Him to them. [5] And

> they were glad, and agreed to give him money. [6] So he promised and sought opportunity to betray Him to them in the absence of the multitude. (Luk 22:3-6 NKJ)

Scripture clearly points out that Judas's concern for the poor went only as far as ensuring he received his elitist cut of the monies.

So the pointed questions for us today become, "Are we betraying Christ by aligning ourselves with those who feign a concern for the poor while benefiting themselves with financial and political power? Are we going to betray Christ and our obligations for individual giving by foisting upon others our obligations? Are we going to empower the very ones who would control us in their zeal to bypass God's workings in the heart? Will we allow politicians to show themselves superior to God by bringing "salvation" to the masses with the tax money plundered from others? It happened to Judas Iscariot who lived with Christ day by day!

The godless mock the church for its failures, but no one will go to Hell for their failures. God knows we will all fail; He intentionally has the back-up plan already established by Jesus Christ redeeming us on the cross. Only those who cannot confess their wayward path (i.e., sins) and will not change due to their selfish and prideful ways will be lost in Hell.

In Revelation, the term beast in all its different manifestations of kingdoms, symbols, horns, and persons (i.e., Anti-Christ) is actually quite descriptive of a vast army of mindless government bureaucrats who do the bidding of the dragon (i.e., Satan), who have seared their consciences to the point that the burning and gassing of Jews or the beheading of Christians is of no concern.

> Now the Spirit expressly says that in latter times some will depart from the faith, giving heed to deceiving spirits and doctrines of demons, [2] speaking lies in hypocrisy, having their own conscience seared with a hot iron, (1Ti 4:1-2 NKJ)

Could we as Christians be so naïve, so conscience deadened that we would vote into power the government "beast" to dominate our lives? Would we sell our souls for a promised healthcare or other social program that our own forefathers lived happily without only a few decades ago? Will our forefathers look at us in disgust that we have sold the freedom they suffered for in exchange for a "magic government pill"? The sad thing is that the pill, the progress, the technical advancement came not from the government beast but from "the freedom our forefathers gave us from the beast". We were set free from feudal, elitist lords who would promise us protection, but steal our best hopes and dreams – have we returned to this slavery?

Socialism's Remorse

I wonder if Judas's intentions were up to a point noble, as if by forcing the hand of Jesus through betrayal that somehow Jesus would throw-off the corrupt Jewish leadership and defeat the Roman government to establish a golden millennial kingdom. Does not socialism seek to also force the hand of God to create a golden earthly kingdom? However, after Judas saw what he had done and how his one chance to "solve the world's problems" was gone, then he was overcome with sorrow. Instead of seeking God's forgiveness he commits suicide thus even in death giving Satan the victory in his life. He just did not understand God's grace through Jesus Christ!

> Then Judas, His betrayer, seeing that He had been condemned, was remorseful and brought back the thirty pieces of silver to the chief priests and elders, [4]
> saying, "I have sinned by betraying innocent blood." And they said, "What *is that* to us? You see *to it*!"
> [5] Then he threw down the pieces of silver in the temple and departed, and went and hanged himself. (Mat 27:3-5 NKJ)

It is important to note that we are all subject to Satan's temptation and deception in our thought life. Even Peter was rebuked by Jesus with the words "Get behind Me, Satan! For you are not mindful of the things of God, but the things of men." (Mar 8:33 NKJ) . The key difference is whether we hold onto these thoughts and thus make them our own or do we follow the admonitions of scripture "casting down arguments and every high thing that exalts itself against the knowledge of God, bringing every thought into captivity to the obedience of Christ, (2Co 10:5 NKJ). However, Judas had made this plan of Satan literally part of his self-image. John 13:2 reports that the "Devil now having put into the heart of Judas Iscariot....." to betray Jesus. Biblically speaking one can view our heart as literally our self-image, <u>who we think we are</u>.

Obviously, Judas's betrayal of Christ was planned outside the obedience to Christ because he was disappointed in Christ; yet Christ knew! God for that matter knows all of our disappointments, yet it is in our worship of God in spite of the earthly challenges that most glorifies God and most profoundly refutes the key accusation of Satan that we serve God only for his benefits.

> So Satan answered the LORD and said, "Does Job fear God for nothing? "Have You not made a hedge

> around him, around his household, and around all that he has on every side? You have blessed the work of his hands, and his possessions have increased in the land. (Job 1:9-10 NKJ)

If we worship God only for what He provides us (via some kind of divine socialist paradise), then I would ask "Of what value are we to God's glory in the heavenly court of judgment between God and Satan, the accuser of the brethren? Satan, literally means accuser or adversary.

Satan Entering the Heart of Obama

I would ask this question, "If Barack Obama was wounded to near death and suffered agonizing consequences, do you think he would bring every thought into captivity to the obedience of Christ? Does he even attempt to have any Biblical guidance now? How easily would Satan be able to control him, especially if in his "mind/heart" he was given justification for unmitigated evil?"

Barack Obama and his elitist cohorts are classic postmodernists who essentially scoff at absolute definitions of right and wrong morality. Ken Samples in "A World of Difference" compares some of the key characteristics of the Postmodernists belief system to Christian Theists:[8]

Two Competing Views of Truth

Christian Theists	**Postmodernists**
Truth is:	**Truth is:**
Objective	Subjective
Absolute	Relative
Knowable	Unknowable
Discovered	Invented
Correspondent to Reality	What is useful & workable
The proper object of life's pursuit	Less important than power

The point of these comparisons is to simply state that the United States of America has elected a leadership that has no foundation in truth, but rather specializes in using the persuasive power of language for their own pursuit of power, influence, and pleasure. Does not this description of Postmodernists fit the Lawless One [Anti-Christ] described below?

> And then the lawless one [Anti-Christ] will be revealed, whom the Lord will consume with the breath of His mouth and destroy with the brightness of His coming. The coming of the *lawless one* is according to the working of Satan, with all power, signs, and lying wonders, and with all unrighteous deception among those who perish, because they did not receive the love of the truth, that they might

> be saved. And for this reason God will send them strong delusion, that they should believe the lie, that they all may be condemned who did not believe the truth but had pleasure in unrighteousness. (2Th 2:8 - 12 NKJ)

These are surely “the times that try men’s souls”. However, I believe that the key point of “trial” is whether we either have or do not have the ability to admit we are wrong! Therefore, we need to get back to God’s pure Word to simply ask God to point out where we have failed Him in understanding His ways and His plans for He is “just and able to forgive”.

> If we confess our sins, He is faithful and just to forgive us *our* sins and to cleanse us from all unrighteousness. If we say that we have not sinned, we make Him a liar, and His word is not in us. (1Jo 1:9-10 NKJ)

Chapter 4

Isaiah 18
The Destruction of America

My Isaiah 18 Background

When I was in my early thirties I heard a pastor teach on Isaiah 18. At the conclusion of the reading he stated to the effect, "This chapter ending with all this destruction and corpses numbered beyond burial is a message about a nation that contains substantial numbers of Godly people, because God will only bring the souls of Godly people to his abode – heaven (as stated in the last verse of Isaiah 18)." Therefore, with America being the most Christianized nation I tucked away this Isaiah 18 message for decades. I have often reviewed the message over the years especially in regards to its key features such as the timing of this destruction. Verse 5 describes the time as when this nation's "fruit has ripened and started to spoil" thus indicating a nation just beyond the peak of its spiritual fruit.

Of course, my spirit groaned within me to see the recent election of Barack Obama as President. At that point in time I decided that the warning signs were significant enough that I should take Hebrew at a seminary to ascertain for myself if in fact the message of Isaiah 18 was about America. Additionally, there were certain words that in my comparison of the different translations varied greatly. Therefore, it was important to evaluate if the best English translation word or phrase was used, since a direct word for word translation is not always possible. Without faulting other Hebrew to English translations I think it is important to keep in mind that because of my special interest here I was able to focus in on dedicated searches where others may have been tasked with translating larger sections of the scripture and did not or could not spend the extra intensive translation time and effort on only Isaiah 18. I will document my revisions to the New King James version at the end of this chapter hopefully with sufficient detail to also satisfy the great majority of Hebrew academics and scholars.

I certainly appreciate the King James versions in general because they maintain a close "word for word" approach to translation without trying to over smooth the translation for current day vernacular which can introduce errors in translation over the course of history. In other words, its priority is on translation accuracy over ease of modern day communication. Of course, the Hebrew Scriptures themselves trace back for centuries. The book of Isaiah has been extremely well preserved through the centuries as confirmed by the near perfect match with the Dead Sea scrolls which date untouched to the time of Jesus. Thus it is fortunate that we are working with the book of Isaiah which is one of the best preserved documents in history to the point that it is featured on display at the Shrine of the Book in Israel.

As I examined the original Hebrew Scriptures in Isaiah I found further confirming, non-contradictory, clear evidence that this Isaiah 18 text does readily match the description, history, and character of the United States of America today. Having stated the background for my research I present below my translation of the Hebrew **bold** and *italicized* and my exegesis of the text in normal font. The Hebrew translation will sound somewhat rough to the reader, but I have done this in order to stay as close to the Hebrew "word for word" translation as possible along the same approach as the King James Bible.

Verse 1 - ***Ho! Land of the winged spear which is beyond the rivers of Cush,***

This is the "Ho! or Ah!" of delight as if the artist is turning to one of his favorite creations to present a masterpiece to an appreciating audience.

What is a winged spear?

If you were Isaiah, the prophet, in the 6th century B.C. and you were shown a future vision of an F-15 Eagle fighter aircraft with missile (i.e., spear) armaments, what would you call it?

What nation is symbolized by an eagle?

The eagle literally spears its fish prey from the surface of the water in mid-flight.

The American eagle with spears in its grasp is on our money and national seals.

Therefore, as unusual as it sounds the description of the United States of America as "the land of the winged spear" fits in many ways.

As kids we all described the strangest of lands as being "beyond deepest, darkest Africa" with exotic names like "Timbuktu" which was beyond our limited childlike understanding of geography. Here the prophet is likewise describing this land as "beyond the rivers of Africa" so I think we are safe to include beyond the Atlantic Ocean also given the limited geographic knowledge of Isaiah's day.

Verse 2 - *who is causing to send idols by sea and by implements of paper upon the face of the waters, "You (plural) go swift messengers to a Gentile nation, who is delayed and who causes to be rashly independent, to a people who are to be feared from who they are then and from then after, a Gentile nation (of foreign tongues) "qaw qaw" who tramples down, whose land the rivers divide.*

America has spent its freedom on commercialism (idols of cars, houses, wealth, etc.) instead of attending to God's ways. Unfortunately, we have the world enamored with "things" via our media instead of the blessings of God.

The prophet calls for swift messengers to go to this people who are "delayed" or late in the timing of the world's history – another sign of the end times.

We are also noted for our independence which is good for individual freedoms, but our rashly independent behavior and influence to even cause others to act outside the bounds of God's plans is to our disgrace. The Hebrew verb for "rashly independent" is the same as used to describe Balaam's behavior when he repeatedly tested God with his desires to curse Israel for the gain of wealth from the Moabites. The Angel was prepared to slay Balaam for his "rashly independent" behavior (Numbers 22:32), but his donkey was able to save him from death. Do we seek God or do we seek what is financially expedient (by shifting the national debt to our children)?

We are a people who are to be feared since defeating the British Empire at its founding and then after by becoming the most powerful nation on earth. The people of America are a Gentile nation of a foreign tongue which sounds like "gibberish" to the prophet. The "qaw qaw" is essentially akin to our "blah blah" when we are describing an unknown language.

We are a nation who has trampled, defeated the last few empires of threat to the world – Nazi Germany, Imperial Japan, and Communist Russia.

This nation is blessed not just by one river such as the Jordan for Israel, Nile for Egypt, Euphrates/Tigris for Babylon, but rather by multiple rivers like the Mississippi, Ohio, Tennessee, Missouri, Colorado, Columbia, etc.

Verse 3 – *All you who dwell (the) world and you who inhabit the earth, as a banner is raised (on) mountains, you look!, and as the striking (blowing of) a trumpet, you listen!*

PAY ATTENTION WORLD!

All the world is put on notice by God that when this flag, this symbol is displayed that they are to <u>look</u> just like our Star-Spangled Banner Anthem whose words are:

Oh, say can you <u>see</u> by the dawn's early light

What so proudly we hailed at the twilight's last gleaming?

Whose broad stripes and bright stars thru the perilous fight,

O'er the ramparts we <u>watched</u> were so gallantly streaming?

And the rocket's red glare, the bombs bursting in air,

Gave proof through the night that our flag was still there.

Oh, say does that star-spangled banner yet wave

O'er the land of the free and the home of the brave?

Given this verse and the verses below of destruction I cannot help but see the vision of a land devastated like a tornado blast with only the irony of the Star-Spangled Banner's lonely tune breaking through the eerie quietness and silence of abandonment. Even this nation's National Anthem is rooted in the concepts of Isaiah 18 – a banner/ flag, war and destruction against freedom, and the cry for the world to "See!"

Verse 4 – ***Because, thus says the Lord to me, "I will indeed have peace and I will indeed cause (them) to gaze intently into My abode***

like the warm, dazzling in front of the light of day (and) like a dew cloud in warm harvest."

God tells the prophet that he will indeed cause many of the people of this nation to see His abode (i.e, Heaven) with all of its dawning brilliance and its comforts of beautiful clouds! God uses a similar combination of dazzling light and refreshing rain for His "ecstasy of happiness" expression in 2 Samuel 23:3 – 4.

The God of Israel said, The Rock of Israel spoke to me:

`He who rules over men *must be* just,

Ruling in the fear of God.

And *he shall be* like the light of the morning *when* the sun rises,

A morning without clouds,

Like the tender grass *springing* out of the earth,

By clear shining after rain.' (2Sa 23:3-4 NKJ)

This is describing from God's viewpoint the celebration of the harvest of Godly souls into His eternal kingdom!

America – this is as close as it gets to a rapture before the tribulation! For when the nuclear holocaust occurs there will be many Christians who in the blink of an eye will perish and be with the Lord! Note this is not "the" rapture that occurs at the end of the age after the Anti-Christ has positioned himself for world domination and the beheadings of those who refuse to receive the mark of the beast are occurring. It is beyond the scope of this book to explain and answer all the questions and misconceptions about "the rapture", therefore, I refer the reader to "A Case for Amillenialism – Understanding the End Times" by Dr. Kim Riddlebarger.[9] Dr. Riddlebarger holds a PhD from Fuller Seminary and is a visiting professor of systematic theology at Westminster Theological Seminary in California. In essence, contrary to current popular beliefs there is no "Get Out of Tribulation Free" card for the entire church. Rather Amillenialism has been the "predominant eschatological (end times) view of Christianity since the days of Augustine". As Riddlebarger states, "The millennium is the period of time between the two advents of our Lord with the thousand years of Revelation 20 being symbolic of the entire interadvental age."[10] Satan's is bound by Christ victory at the cross and he is restrained wherever the gospel is preached.

Verse 5 – *Because towards the face of harvest as the flowering bud is hot and unripe fruit is ripening, it will happen the blossom and the shoots are cut off with vine-knives and with the tendrils/ offshoots he causes to get rid of and he causes to break off.*

The timing of the harvest of this nation will be when it has reached its peak and is starting to sour – as if God does not desire to see the agony of a long drawn out collapse for this nation.

Verse 6 – *They will be abandoned together to birds of prey on the mountains and to animals of the land. And the birds of prey summer (i.e., harvest) upon it, And all animals of the land winter (i.e., strip) upon it.*

The death and destruction of this nation will be so great that no one will be there to bury the bodies. Rather the birds and animals of the field will engorge themselves upon the carcasses.

NOTE: Revelations 16:17 through 19:9 goes to great length to describe the destruction of Babylon the Great during the end times. John Price has written "The End of America" based on the conclusion that America is the Whore of Babylon.[11] I must admit that secular America, particularly the media does fit the description of a nation that is "selling its secular religion" and it does vie for the "one voice" communication control portrayed by the original Babylon where scripture states:

> [4] And they said, "Come, let us build ourselves a city, and a tower whose top *is* in the heavens; let us make a name for ourselves, lest we be scattered abroad over the face of the whole earth." [5] But the LORD came down to see the city and the tower which the sons of men had built. [6] And the LORD said, "Indeed the people *are* one and they all have one language, and this is what they begin to do; now nothing that they propose to do will be withheld from them. [7] "Come, let Us go down and there confuse their language, that they may not understand one another's speech." [8] So the LORD scattered them

> abroad from there over the face of all the earth, and they ceased building the city. [9] Therefore its name is called Babel, because there the LORD confused the language of all the earth; and from there the LORD scattered them abroad over the face of all the earth. (Gen 11:4-9 NKJ)

The end of these verses in Revelation about Babylon's destruction also coincidentally mentions the "marriage supper of the Lamb" which ties with the Bride of Christ as also described below in Isaiah 18. Therefore, the Destruction of America, with its godly Christian population and the Destruction of the Whore of Babylon, the secularly-bound population are not mutually exclusive events. I believe John Price has brought out an important point here about how well the secularists including America fit the description of the Whore of Babylon. The only descriptive feature of the Whore of Babylon that may be a challenge to fit is her guilt for being "drunken with the blood of the saints"; however, we do not yet know what escalating persecutions against Christians the secular society may bring to bear during the end times and, of course, there is the national tragedy of abortion.

In further agreement within these same Revelation verses is the description of "who" destroys the Whore of Babylon.

> "And the ten horns which you saw on the beast, these will hate the harlot, make her desolate and naked, eat her flesh and burn her with fire. (Rev 17:16 NKJ)

Joel Richardson in his book "The Islamic Anti-Christ"[12] points out that this beast is essentially a revived Islamic Empire. No wonder this beast hates the secular Whore of Babylon. The last and Seventh kingdom to rule over Jerusalem was Islamic and this eighth beast and final beast will be from the Seventh kingdom as shown below.

> "Here *is* the mind which has wisdom: The seven heads are seven mountains on which the woman sits. **(America dominates all seven continents)** [10] "There are also seven kings. Five have fallen **(Egypt, Assyria, Babylon, Persia, Greece)** , one is **(Rome)**, *and* the other has not yet come **(Islam)**. And when he comes, he must continue a short time. [11] "And the beast that was, and is not, is himself also the eighth **(Islam)**, and is of the seven **(Islam)**, and is going to perdition. [12] "The ten horns which you saw are ten kings who have received no kingdom as yet, but they receive authority for one hour as kings with the beast. [13] "These are of one mind, and they will give their power and authority to the beast. (Rev 17:9-13 NKJ)

In summary, the Islamic "one world government " beast will arise to destroy the secular Whore of Babylon, America. This scriptural testimony from multiple and independent viewpoints is additional confirming evidence that America is doomed to destruction as described by Isaiah 18.

Verse 7 – *At that time, "the she" gift will be caused to be brought to the Lord of Hosts, a portion (of) people, who is delayed and who causes to be rashly independent, to a people who are to be feared from who they are then and from then after, a Gentile nation (of foreign tongues) "qaw qaw" who tramples down, whose land the*

rivers divide --- to (the) place of the name of the Lord of Hosts --- Mount Zion.

At the time of this great destruction and loss of life "**THE SHE**" gift to the Lord will be <u>caused</u> to be brought ..... (God is in control to bring about these events!). This gift in the Hebrew is "the", as in "the" definite article; not "a" as in the indefinite article. The Hebrew follows the definite "the" with the singular feminine pronoun, i.e., "she". Thus in describing this gift it is specifically called "**THE SHE** gift" – and of course **THE Church is the "Bride of Christ"! Amen!**

The description of this people is repeated exactly as above in verse 2 for emphasis. Even the Hebrew repetition is exactly the same.

The gift to the Lord is a <u>portion</u> of these people from the destroyed nation who will go to the place of the name of the Lord ----- to Mount Zion (which is symbolic of the worshipping church)!

> But you have come to Mount Zion and to the city of the living God, the heavenly Jerusalem, to an innumerable company of angels, to the general assembly and church of the firstborn *who are* registered in heaven, to God the Judge of all, to the spirits of just men made perfect, to Jesus the Mediator of the new covenant, and to the blood of sprinkling that speaks better things than *that of* Abel. (Heb 12:22 - 24 NKJ)

Key Translation Comparisons with New King James Bible

The section will present a comparison of the key words used by the New King James version with an alternative English translation that is directly possible using conventional word choices. These translation word choices are from the same Hebrew/English lexicons used throughout main stream Bible seminaries. In other words, these translations are supported by Biblical scholars. Just like in English where the same word can mean quite different things such as:

a) "fair" lady

b) "fair" deal

c) county "fair"

Then, likewise Hebrew has similar duplicate word usage issues which may be even more so given that it is an ancient language, not distant from the beginnings of writing, and it has not had as much tendency as English to adopt new words from other languages. Therefore, whenever there are curious verses in the Old Testament that do not seem to make sense one should do the research (ideally in Hebrew) to resolve such matters. Often one can find usage of the same Hebrew word in another verse; thus providing good support for the word usage in the verse in question. The words in **bold** below are therefore provided with specific verses as examples where the Hebrew context demonstrates a clear usage in support of these translations for Isaiah 18.

God desires us to study the scriptures:

> These were more fair-minded than those in Thessalonica, in that they received the word with all

> readiness, and searched the Scriptures daily *to find out* whether these things were so. [12] Therefore many of them believed, and also not a few of the Greeks, prominent women as well as men. [13] But when the Jews from Thessalonica learned that the word of God was preached by Paul at Berea, they came there also and stirred up the crowds. (Act 17:11-13 NKJ)

However, he also points out that there will be those who will fight even God rather than admit that their particular understanding of scripture is flawed.

Verse 1

Isaiah 18:1 **Woe** to the land **shadowed with buzzing wings**, which *is* beyond the rivers of **Ethiopia,**

Ho! *Land of the winged* ***spear*** *which is beyond the rivers of* ***Cush,***

a) ***Ho!***

הוֹי – interjection: A. alas! woe! (e.g., I King 13:30), B. ho! (encouraging, inciting e.g., Isaiah 18:1, Zechariah 2:10)

b) ***spear***

צְלָצַל – (construct state of) spear A. Can you fill his skin with harpoons, Or his head with fishing spears? (e.g., Job 41:7), or B. cricket (e.g., Deuteronomy 28:42)

c) ***Cush***

כּוּשׁ – ancient name of land encompassing today's Ethiopia

(NOTE: Isaiah would not have been able to describe all of Africa, since it was beyond the geographical understandings of his day)

Verse 2

Isaiah 18:2 Which sends **ambassadors** by sea,
Even in **vessels** of **reed** on the waters, ***saying,***
"**Go**, swift messengers, to a **nation tall and smooth of *skin,***
To a **people terrible** from their beginning onward,
A nation powerful and **treading down**,
Whose land the rivers divide."

*who is causing to send **idols** by sea and by **implements** of **paper** upon the face of the waters, **(God commanding) "You (plural) go** swift messengers to a **Gentile nation, who is delayed and who causes to be rashly independent**, to a people **who are to be feared** from who they are then and from then after, a **Gentile nation (of foreign tongues) "qaw qaw" who tramples down,** whose land the rivers divide.*

a) ***idols***

צִירִים – a *form* (of beauty; as if *pressed* out, that is, carved); hence an (idolatrous) *image:* - beauty, idol (e.g., Isaiah 45:16)

b) ***implements***

כְּלֵי – useful object in the widest sense:-- 1. Vessel, receptacle, gear: in general (e.g., Gen 31:37); 2. equipment, gear (e.g., Gen 45:20); 3. Implement (e.g., Gen 49:5)

c) ***paper***

גֹּמֶא – papyrus, (e.g, Isaiah 35:7, Exodus 2:3)

d) ***(God commanding) "You (plural) go***

לְכוּ – 1. go - imperative command 2nd person masculine plural (הלך) (e.g., Gen 12:1)

e) ***Gentile nation***

גּוֹי – nation (used principally for non-Israel peoples) (e.g, Ex 34:24)

f) ***who is delayed***

מְמֻשָּׁךְ – verb pual participle masculine singular absolute of put off, delayed (משך)(e.g, Proverbs 13:12...Hope deferred makes the heart sick, But *when* the desire comes, *it is* a tree of life. (NKJ))

g) ***who causes to be rashly independent***

מוֹרָט – hifil participle masculine singular absolute of to be rashly independent (ירט) (e.g, Numbers 22:32, Job 16:11)

NOTE: Hifil is a "causative" verb tense, thus the USA is an influence toward independence, democracy, a change in culture, etc.

h) ***who are to be feared***

נוֹרָא – verb niphal participle masculine singular absolute homonym of to be feared, reverenced, held in high honor (ירא)(e.g, Psalms 130:4, Exodus 15:11)

i) ***"qaw qaw"***

קַו־קָו – syllable indicating prophetic speech or an unknown tongue (e.g., Isaiah 28:10-13)

j) ***who tramples down***

מְבוּסָה –noun common feminine singular absolute participle

trampling (e.g., Isaiah 22:5)

Verse 3

Isaiah 18:3 All inhabitants of the world and dwellers on the earth:
When he lifts up a banner on the mountains, you see *it;*
And when he blows a trumpet, you hear *it.*

All you who dwell (the) world and you who inhabit the earth, as a banner is raised (on) mountains, you look!, and as the striking (blowing of) a trumpet, you listen!

Verse 4

Isaiah 18:4 For so the LORD said to me,
"I will take My rest,
And I will look from My dwelling place
Like clear heat in sunshine,
Like a cloud of dew in the heat of harvest."
Because, thus says the Lord to me,

*"I will indeed have peace and **I will indeed cause (them) to gaze intently into My abode** like the warm, dazzling in front of the light of day (and) like a dew cloud in warm harvest."*

a) ***I will indeed cause (them) to gaze intently***

אַבִּיטָה – verb hiphil imperfect 1st person common singular cohortative of נבט 1. look in a specific direction: a) with a word of direction, to the heavens in Gen 15:5, b) look out, gaze (e.g., Isaiah 63:15)

NOTE: Hifil is a "causative" verb tense, thus God is causing someone to gaze

b) ***into My abode***

בִּמְכוֹנִי -

i. בּ – preposition with basic meaning of local and instrumental relationship (e.g., in the eyes of, Gen 16:4, 2. within your gates, Exodus 20:10, 3. on the 7th day, Gen 2:2, 4. into shadow of my roof Genesis 19:8

NOTE: The Hebrew letter "bet - ב " indicates in, into, within whereas the Hebrew letter "mem - מ " is required to indicate from. Therefore, God is causing someone to gaze into His abode, rather than God, Himself gazing from His abode.

ii. מְכוֹן – foundation, set there upon her own base (e.g., Zechariah 5:11), abode, a settled place for thee to abide (e.g, I Kings 8:13), place (to set it up in his place (e.g., Ezra 2:68)

iii. ִי – 1st person singular suffix – my, of me

Verse 5

Isaiah 18:5 For before the harvest, when the bud is perfect
And the sour grape is ripening in the flower,
He will both cut off the sprigs with pruning hooks
And take away *and* cut down the branches.

Because towards the face of harvest as the flowering bud is hot and unripe fruit is ripening, it will happen the blossom and the shoots are cut off with vine-knives and with the tendrils/offshoots he causes to get rid of and he causes to break off.

NOTE: The picture here of a harvest occurring at the full ripening time "of this nation" is clear; the original unsmoothed Hebrew translation is simply at little bit rougher sounding to the English listener.

Verse 6

Isaiah 18:6 They will be left together for the mountain birds of prey
And for the beasts of the earth;
The birds of prey will summer on them,
And all the beasts of the earth will winter on them.

They will be abandoned together to birds of prey on the mountains and to animals of the land.
And the birds of prey summer (harvest) upon it,
And all animals of the land winter (strip) upon it.

Verse 7

Isaiah 18:7 In that time **a** present **will be brought** to the LORD of hosts,

........(Repetition of the content of verse 2 exactly for emphasis)......

To the place of the name of the LORD of hosts, To Mount Zion.

At that time, ***the (she)*** *gift* ***will be caused to***

be brought to the Lord of Hosts, a portion (of) people, ...

.....(Repetition of the content of verse 2 exactly for emphasis).........

--- to (the) place of the name of the Lord of Hosts --- Mount Zion.

a) ***the***

הַ – definite article, "the" (as opposed to the indefinite article,

"a")

b) ***(she)***

הִיא – feminine singular pronoun – she , 1. that she *was* very beautiful (e.g., Gen 12:14)

c) ***will be caused to be brought***

יוּבַל -- verb hophal imperfect 3rd person masculine singular of to be brought (יבל) 1. He is caused to be brought as a lamb to the slaughter (e.g, Isaiah 53:7), 2. be led forth with peace (e.g., Isaiah 55:12), 3. With gladness and rejoicing shall they be brought (e.g., Psalms 45:15)

NOTE: Hofal is a "passive causative" verb tense, thus this gift of a portion of people are being caused to be brought to God (and obviously by God).

Chapter 5
Now what?

Recap of Scriptural Revelations

In this book we have unveiled the following mysteries which were concealed in scripture until this present age:

1) The name Barack Obama, the 44th President of the United States, is called out by Jesus as being Satan at his fall. The persona linked with Satan at his ultimate fall is the Man of Lawlessness or commonly called the Anti-Christ.

2) The original betrayer of Jesus Christ was Judas Iscariot, who expressly proclaimed his disappointment with Jesus for not using a certain expensive ointment as cash for the poor. This socialistic rage against Jesus, who is God in the flesh, is consistent with

the ultimate number of the Anti-Christ led government Beast, 666. The number of the Beast is the number of humanity, since Adam was created on the 6th day. The 666 symbolizes the trinity of humanity as if man's socialistic plans can save himself. Barack Obama is the world's most powerful socialist leader.

3) Isaiah chapter 18 prophesies the destruction of a nation which closely matches the unique characteristics of the United States of America with 16 different aspects as follows:

a) Winged spear – most advanced military aircraft, eagle as national symbol

b) A land beyond Africa (i.e., the New World)

c) A nation that is influencing others via idols (e.g., consumerism, Hollywood)

d) A nation that dominates the world of communications and business as symbolized by its implements of paper (i.e., news media, technical documents)

e) A Gentile (non-Jewish) nation

f) A nation of people who arrive on the world stage late in history

g) A people known for being rashly independent

h) A people who are to be feared from their beginning and thereafter (i.e., defeat of British Empire to ultimately become the world superpower)

i) A people of a foreign language unknown to the Hebrews (i.e., English)

j) A nation who dominates others (i.e., WWII, Cold War, Iraq)

k) A land that is blessed with several major rivers

l) A nation that upon its destruction will call for world-wide attention

m) A nation that is not yet, but approaching decline

n) A nation that is so advanced and specialized that a nuclear attack disruption of its society will bring about millions of unburied corpses

o) A nation with large numbers of Christians who upon their death will be brought into God's presence in heaven

p) The ones brought into God's presence are described as "THE SHE" gift which is the description of the Church as the Bride of Christ.

Eschatology Implications

The purpose of this book is not to revise and/or correct all the variety of end times interpretations that are out there. Rather this book presents a small yet powerful vignette regarding three specific questions of the end times which are:

A. Who is the Anti-Christ?

Barack Obama

B. How does the number clue 666 relate to the Anti-Christ?

> Man was created on the 6th day thus 666 represents the trinity of humanity which is expressed by the "socialism salvation" deception so prevalent in today's world.

C. What about the United States in the end times?

> Isaiah 18 prophesies that the United States of America will be destroyed with great death and destruction, but one specific positive result that is mentioned to occur concurrently is the great harvest of many as The Church, The Bride of Christ.

I have no desire to battle every end times expert over the details of every scriptural interpretation. In fact, for many if not the majority of end times scenarios these specific points of scriptural insight elaborated herein are quite compatible with their assessments. In summary, I personally am well satisfied with the end times scenarios described in "A Case for Amillenialism" by Dr. Kim Riddlebarger. Likewise, the book "The Man of Sin" by Dr. Riddlebarger is excellent in how it demonstrates that very few requirements are needed to provide the set up for "The Anti-Christ". For example, there is no requirement for the rebuilding of the Temple in Jerusalem where the Anti-Christ can declare himself God, since the temple (ναὸν) of 2 Thessalonians 2:4 is the same Greek word used for temple in I Corinthians 3:9-17 which states:

> For we are God's fellow workers; you are God's field, <u>*you are* God's building</u>. [10] According to the grace of God which was given to me, <u>as a wise master builder I have laid the foundation</u>, and <u>another builds on it</u>. But let each one take heed how he builds on it. [11]

> For no other foundation can anyone lay than that which is laid, which is Jesus Christ. [12] Now if anyone builds on this foundation *with* gold, silver, precious stones, wood, hay, straw, [13] each one's work will become clear; for the Day will declare it, because it will be revealed by fire; and the fire will test each one's work, of what sort it is. [14] If anyone's work which he has built on *it* endures, he will receive a reward. [15] If anyone's work is burned, he will suffer loss; but he himself will be saved, yet so as through fire. [16] Do you not know that you are the temple of God and *that* the Spirit of God dwells in you? [17] If anyone defiles the temple of God, God will destroy him. For the temple of God is holy, which *temple* you are. (1Cor 3:9 NKJ)

Therefore, once the veil of the Temple was torn upon Jesus crucifixion, the Jewish temple was no longer "God's" temple, rather the Church, we became God's temple. And when the AntiChrist speaking in God's temple, the Church, defiles it with his blasphemies he will be destroyed!

Our Conduct

The advice to Christians today need be no different than that to the Christians of Paul's day when he too advised them of the imminent coming of the Lord. In 1st Thessalonians chapters 4 - 5 Paul prescribes that our behavior is to be as Godly diligent workers until the end with circumspect behavior that continues to glorify God. May we all likewise follow this Godly counselor.

Our Only Hope

I must humbly admit that I have no physical solutions that I can recommend to save America from its God given destiny on the world stage, but I do have a spiritual solution that is offered to all in Jesus Christ. The verses below illustrate how a nation that missed the Promised One of God exchanging Him for a murderer (i.e., Barabbas, the rebel) can still be redeemed. Have we become a nation that sits as cripples waiting for the alms of government hand outs rather than leaping and praising God? May we likewise repent, be converted, and enjoy times of refreshing before the end times restoration of all things as promised by God through His holy prophets.

> Then Peter said, "Silver and gold I do not have, but what I do have I give you: In the name of Jesus Christ of Nazareth, rise up and walk." [7] And he took him by the right hand and lifted *him* up, and immediately his feet and ankle bones received strength. [8] So he, leaping up, stood and walked and entered the temple with them-- walking, leaping, and praising God. [9] And all the people saw him walking and praising God. [10] Then they knew that it was he who sat begging alms at the Beautiful Gate of the temple; and they were filled with wonder and amazement at what had happened to him. [11] Now as the lame man who was healed held on to Peter and John, all the people ran together to them in the porch which is called Solomon's, greatly amazed. [12] So when Peter saw *it*, he responded to the people: "Men of Israel, why do you marvel at this? Or why look so intently

at us, as though by our own power or godliness we
had made this man walk? [13] "The God of Abraham,
Isaac, and Jacob, the God of our fathers, glorified His
Servant Jesus, whom you delivered up and denied
in the presence of Pilate, when he was determined
to let *Him* go. [14] "But you denied the Holy One and
the Just, and asked for a murderer to be granted
to you, [15] "and killed the Prince of life, whom God
raised from the dead, of which we are witnesses. [16]
"And His name, through faith in His name, has made
this man strong, whom you see and know. Yes, the
faith which *comes* through Him has given him this
perfect soundness in the presence of you all. [17] "Yet
now, brethren, I know that you did *it* in ignorance, as
did also your rulers. [18] "But those things which God
foretold by the mouth of all His prophets, that the
Christ would suffer, He has thus fulfilled. [19] "Repent
therefore and be converted, that your sins may be
blotted out, so that times of refreshing may come
from the presence of the Lord, [20] "and that He may
send Jesus Christ, who was preached to you before,
[21] "whom heaven must receive until the times of
restoration of all things, which God has spoken by
the mouth of all His holy prophets since the world
began. (Act 3:6-21 NKJ)

AUTHOR BIOGRAPHY

Stephen Kirk is an engineering consultant of 25+ years experience in the Oil & Gas industry and a graduate student in Christian Apologetics.

At the age of 12 I accepted Christ as my Savior. The critical moment occurred during the hot, humid days of a June vacation Bible school in a small southern town. As the pastor over the previous weeks and months proclaimed the heart-wrenching sacrifice that Christ had made for me and all of His family I reached the point of casting off that demonic lie of "what will others say when you admit you are a sinner". I believe that moment shaped my character from that day forward such that to this day I am not haunted by such voices of fear and concealing darkness. I am called therefore to announce those things that are publicly unpopular.

I believe if I had refused to choose Christ at that young age I too would have become just another naysayer and cynic jeering those who would step out for God and truth. My favorite saint of the Bible is Stephen who testified even to the point of martyrdom. (Acts 6:5- 8:1)

Appendix A

Key Hebrew word translations of Luke 10:18

For a small donation of $25 anyone can have access to e-Sword www.e-sword.net a Bible software with Strong's Concordance linked to the Hebrew text as listed below. For the price of ~$350 one can acquire BibleWorks 8 www.bibleworks.com which is the premier original languages Bible software program for Biblical exegesis and research. It comes with Greek, Hebrew, and Septuagint Bibles for your computer, as well as translations in English, German, Spanish, Chinese, Korean, etc. BibleWorks is a tightly integrated collection of Bible software tools, such as Holladay's Lexicon, designed specifically for scholarly analysis of the Bible text. Check the TRUTH yourself!

Strong's Concordance – H1300

ברק

baraq

baw-rawk'

From H1299; *lightning*; by analogy a *gleam*; concretely a *flashing* sword: - bright, glitter (-ing, sword), lightning.

Holladay Lexicon – H1302

בָּרָק noun common masculine singular absolute homonym 1

בָּרָק: cs. בְּרַק; pl. בְּרָקִים, sf. בְּרָקָיו: lightning Ex 19:16

Strong's Concordance – H1116

במה

bamah

baw-maw'

From an unused root (meaning to *be high*); an *elevation:* - height, high place, wave.

Holladay 1120

בָּמָה (ca. 100 x): loc. הַבָּמָתָה 1Sam 9:13; pl. בָּמוֹת, cs. בָּמוֹת (10 x), בָּמוֹתֵי Kt Dt 32:13 Isa 58:14 Mi 1:3, & בָּמֳתֵי (bom°te < sg. * בֹּמֶת) Isa 14:14 Amos 4:13 Job 9:8 & Qr Dt 32:13 Isa 58:14 Mic 1:3; sf. בָּמוֹתַי, בָּמוֹתֵימוֹ, בָּמ(וֹ)תָיו: -- 1.**back** a) Dt 33:29; b) metaph.

Is 14:14, Job 9:8 (backs of the sea); -- 2. (not easily distinguishable from 1b & 3!) mountain ridge, height, a) of land 2 Sam 1:19-25, b) God treads on Amos 4:13; -- 3. **Canaanite burial ground** Ez 43:7; -- 4. (cultic) **high place** (ca. 80 x, esp. in 1 & 2 Kings, 2 Chr) I K 11:7 associated with pagan worship & cultic prostitution.

Conjunctive Vav

וּ

u,oo before a "bet" ב, "mem" מ, "pe" פ

conjunction such as *and, even, in addition*

Holladay 2098

וְ: form: mostly וְ, but a) וּ before ב, מ, & פ, & before cons. with simple *shewa*; b) וָ immediately before tone-syl.: וָבֵ֫יְתָה; c) וַ, וֶ, וָ, (wo) before cons. with corresponding *hatef*: וַאֲנִי; d) וִ before יְ: וִיהִי; e) וַ with *dages forte* & וָ before א in imperfect consecutive; -- 1. **and**, connecting 2 words or phrases

Strong's Concordance – H7482

רעם

ra'am

rah'-am

From H7481; a *peal* of thunder: - thunder.

Holladay – 7992

רַעַם (raam)

רעם: qal: impf. יִרְעַם: subj. sea: **storm, thunder** Ps 96:11 98:7 1Chr 16:32.

hif.: pf. הִרְעִים; impf. יַרְעֵם (: subj. Y.: (cause it to) **thunder, storm** 1 Sam 2:10.

Appendix B

STATISTICAL PROOF OF AN INFINITELY INTELLIGENT DESIGNER

Random chance (i.e., evolution) limits itself to operating by the rules of probabilities; therefore, the chance for a "CERTAIN" arrangement of items (i.e., letters, DNA molecules) is calculated by the formula:

$$\mathbf{P = A^n}$$

where,

P = Probability (average events required to produce "ONE DESIRED ARRANGEMENT")

A = Available choices of items (i.e., letters, DNA molecules coding for amino acids)

n = number of items in the "ONE DESIRED ARRANGEMENT"

For example, if

A = 2 with the letters of choice limited to "I" and "T"

n = 2 for a TWO item arrangement

then, $P = 2^2$

P = 2 x 2

P = 4

which is demonstrated by table below

IT	TT
TI	II

where 1 out of 4 has meaning in this example and the rest are meaningless in English; therefore, there is a 25% chance of meaningful success in this simple example.

For another example, if

A = 3 with the letters of choice limited to "G" — "O" — "D"

n = 3 for a THREE item arrangement

then,

$P = 3^3$

P = 3 x 3 X 3

P = 27

which is demonstrated by the table below

GOD	GGD	**ODD**	DOD	DGD
GOO	GGO	ODO	DOO	DGO
GOG	GGG	ODG	**DOG**	DGG
GDD	OOD	OGD	DDD	
GDO	OOO	OGO	DDO	
GDG	OOG	OGG	DDG	

where 4 out of 27 has meaning in this example and the rest are meaningless in English; therefore, a 15% chance of meaningful success for this slightly more complex example.

When this evolutionary "random chance" analysis is extended to the more complex real world we find that the probabilities of favorable mutations are astronomically impossible, for example:

- Genetic code informational data is like language informational data. English has 26 letters while the genetic code in DNA uses 20 amino acids from which ALL life building instructions are made.

- Given a maximum 500 meaningful 3 letter words in the English language, therefore, $500/26^3$ equals a 1 in 35 successful random chance for word construction.

- Given a maximum 10,000 meaningful 7 letter words in the English language, therefore, $10{,}000/26^7$ equals a 1 in 800,000 successful random chance for word construction.

- A sentence with 100 letters = $10^{25}/ 26^{100} = 1/10^{100}$ probability of a successful 100 letter sentence by random chance (yet there are only 10^{70} atoms in the entire universe!!!!!!!!!!)

YET, PEOPLE ARE CREATORS ALSO BECAUSE WE CAN EASILY WRITE A 100 LETTER SENTENCE IN 60 SECONDS THAT CAN COMMUNICATE WITH ANOTHER HUMAN!

- A bacterium (E. Coli) has a chromosome of 4.7 million DNA base pairs[(1)] with every three base pairs equating to one amino acid (i.e., letter) in the genetic code, therefore, it is the informational equivalent to a 1.5 million letter book (i.e., ~600 page novel). The probability of writing this bacterium's genetic code book by random chance is $1/20^{1.5\text{ million}}$ which is greater than 10 with 1.5 million zeros behind it. The human genetic code is 3 billion DNA base pairs for comparison.

(1) James E. Bailey, *Biochemical Engineering Fundamentals* (McGraw-Hill, 1986) pg. 51.

DO WE GIVE CREDIT TO A DESIGNER OR TO THE RANDOM CHANCE OF EVOLUTION; DO YOU WANT CREDIT FOR YOUR DESIGN WORK OR SHOULD WE GIVE IT TO YOUR PENCIL?

(Endnotes)

[1] Paul D. Wegner, *A Student's Guide to Textual Criticism of the Bible* (InterVarsity Press, 2006) 229-255

[2] George M. Lamsa, *Idioms in the Bible Explained and A Key to The Original Gospels* (HarperCollins Publishers, 1985)

[3] Ibid.

[4] William L. Holladay, *A Concise Hebrew and Aramaic Lexicon of the Old Testament* (William B. Eerdmans Publishing Company, 1988)

[5] Kenneth Richard Samples *A World of Difference – Putting Christian TruthClaims to the Worldview Test* (Baker Publishing Group, 2007) 39-54.

[6] Kim Riddlebarger *The Man of Sin* (Baker Publishing Group 2006) pg. 112

[7] Lyle H. Rossiter, Jr. M.D., *The Liberal Mind- The Psychological Causes of Political Madness* (Free World Books, 2006)

[8] Kenneth Richard Samples *A World of Difference – Putting Christian TruthClaims to the Worldview Test* (Baker Publishing Group 2007) pg. 226

[9] Kim Riddlebarger *A Case for Amillenialism – Understanding the End Times* (Baker Book House Publishing, 2003)

[10] Ibid. pg. 31

[11] John Price *The End of America* (Christian House Publishers, 2009)

[12] Joel Richardson *The Islamic AntiChrist* (WorldNetDaily, 2009)

www.ingramcontent.com/pod-product-compliance
Ingram Content Group UK Ltd.
Pitfield, Milton Keynes, MK11 3LW, UK
UKHW041925190726
13854UKWH00003B/1454